Cambridge English Readers

....

Level 4

Series editor: Philip

A Matter of Chance

David A. Hill

CAMBRIDGE
UNIVERSITY PRESS

CAMBRIDGE UNIVERSITY PRESS

Cambridge, New York, Melbourne, Madrid, Cape Town, Singapore, São Paulo, Delhi

Cambridge University Press
The Edinburgh Building, Cambridge CB2 8RU, UK

www.cambridge.org
Information on this title: www.cambridge.org/9780521775526

First published 1999
10th printing 2008

Printed in China by Sheck Wah Tong Printing Press Limited

A catalogue record for this publication is available from the British Library

ISBN 978-0-521-77552-6 paperback
ISBN 978-0-521-68621-1 paperback plus audio CD pack

Contents

Characters

Paul Morris: a marketing manager for pharmaceutical companies, first in Manchester, England, then in Italy.
Jacky Morris: Paul's wife, a marketing manager for the same pharmaceutical companies.
Sandra Rovello: works for an Italian pharmaceutical company.
Mr and Mrs Rovello: Sandra's parents. Mr Rovello manages an import-export furniture company.
Andrea Carta: a business partner of Mr Rovello's.

N

Manchester

BRITAIN

Newhaven

Dieppe

Paris

FRANCE

Bourges

Clermont
Ferrand

SWITZERLAND

Lugano

Magreglio
Lake Como

Milan

Portofino

ITALY

0   250   500 km

Chapter 1 *The roof-tile*

The roof-tile fell.

******

After two or three hundred years of rain, ice, snow, wind and sun the roof-tile fell.

******

After two or three hundred years of rain, ice, snow, wind and sun the roof-tile fell from its place down into the street of the old town.

******

After two or three hundred years of rain, ice, snow, wind and sun the roof-tile fell from its place down into the street of the old town and hit my wife in the middle of her head.

******

After two or three hundred years of rain, ice, snow, wind and sun the roof-tile fell from its place down into the street of the old town and hit my wife in the middle of her head, killing her instantly.

Chapter 2 *Jacky*

Jacky.

What can I tell you about Jacky?

I can tell you how she looked that bright February morning when she stepped out into the new sun, as the snow was falling off all the roofs, as she went out to buy something for a dress she was making. For a special dinner – we had been married for three years.

I have a film library of her in the back of my head: in the office; our first Christmas together, skiing in Scotland; the wedding; the trip across France to our new home in Italy; and . . . and . . . I also have ten photographs of her that I took. Just ten out of the hundreds.

Afterwards, when I was able to, I looked through all the photos of our life together and carefully chose the ten I liked the best. I then had them enlarged, and put them in a special photo album. Which I have never opened since. All this was many years ago. I am an old man now.

An old man full of memories, and full of thoughts about what could have been. An old man who often thinks about the way that one tiny chance happening can change someone's life: the roof-tile falls a second earlier or a second later, she goes towards a different shop, she goes towards the same shop a different way, she meets a friend and stops to talk, she doesn't meet a friend and stop to talk, the traffic lights change as she gets to the crossing . . . or . . . or . . .

Such a little tiny chance that she was there then and the roof-tile was there then. Such a little tiny chance that left me, at twenty-seven years of age, alone in a foreign country. Italy. So much hope. Such a bright future. Such an exciting thing to do. An adventure. To go and start a new life in Italy.

Jacky and I had met at work in Manchester. We had started at the same time. We enjoyed being together at first because we were both new there, and it was good to have someone in the same situation to talk to. Talk at work led to talk in pubs, days out at weekends, and by November we were in love and planning a first skiing holiday in Scotland . . . the first time together, the first time away with someone I really loved.

After that things moved quickly. We got engaged to be married on her twenty-fourth birthday (January 20) and got married at Easter. We then spent two more years working in Manchester, during which time we decided that we wanted a change. We'd visited Italy twice in those years. Once we'd toured around the northern lakes in a car, and once we'd stayed in a farmhouse in Umbria.

We fell in love with Italy the first moment we got there, for all the usual romantic reasons – the sun, the scenery, the food and wine, the people, the buildings. It seemed right for us. We went to Italian evening classes in Manchester, and got quite good at the language.

'*Io mi chiamo Paul Morris, e tu sei la mia moglie, Jacky*' I used to sing around the house. We watched Italian films at the Arts Centre, and we went to Italian restaurants regularly.

We wanted a change. Three years in Manchester was

enough. Jacky came from Norwich and I came from Bedford, so neither of us had any reason to stay in Manchester except the job and each other. And then that special day came. One Friday evening I was reading the 'Abroad' part of the APPOINTMENTS section in the weekly company newspaper, when one advertisement jumped off the page at me:

CORVO PHARMACEUTICALS

Well-established company in Como needs two enthusiastic young marketing managers to start September 1st.
Accommodation provided.
Return airfare paid.

Tel: Mrs Robinson on
0183-7674321 for further details.

I remember running into the kitchen with the paper shouting 'Jacky! Jacky! Como!' and nearly knocking her down in my excitement.

We'd been to Como two years earlier and we'd loved both the town and the lake. And now here was a job in that wonderful place!

Jacky was soon more excited than me, and phoned Mrs Robinson at once. We couldn't sleep that night, talking about all the wonderful possibilities if we could get the job. The following Monday the application forms and details about the job arrived. It all sounded perfect. The company was a good one, and they provided a flat in the centre of the old town. To cut a long story short, we applied for the jobs, we were given interviews and, in late May, we were offered the jobs. And we accepted.

Italy. We were going to live there. Out of cold wet Manchester and into those hot summers, the blue lake, the snowy winters, the beautiful scenery, the skiing . . . it was all going to be ours all the time!

We left our jobs. Everyone, our friends and family, even the people at work, thought we were silly to leave good jobs in England for an uncertain life abroad. We had expected that. We didn't mind. We packed our things, left some things with our parents and sent other things to Italy by train. In mid-August we took a two-week holiday and drove through France by car on our way to Como.

We arrived at the end of August to get the flat ready before starting work in September. It was three years after we'd met in Manchester. What a lot of changes in such a short time!

Even now, after all these years, I can still remember exactly how good it felt to be in Como. Jacky and Italy, I used to say to myself, the two loves of my life, and I had them both! What a lucky man!

And I knew that Jacky felt just the same. Our love for each other grew stronger. We did everything together. Work and play. We were closer than ever before. We really enjoyed our work. The Italians we worked with were wonderful and we made friends easily. And at home all the neighbours were welcoming and helpful. It all seemed perfect.

And then, five months later, she wasn't there any more. I would never see her grey eyes shining up at me again; her hair on the pillow, like in that song by Leonard Cohen – 'a sleepy golden storm'. Nothing. Just me.

Chapter 3 *Sandra*

What do you do when a big hole suddenly appears in your life? You either fall into it, or you start to fill it up.

Jacky was buried back at home in England. To me, it all seemed to happen in a bad dream. Everything that happened after that seemed like a dream too.

There were a lot of papers to fill in, meetings to go to and trips back to England. But there was one thing clear in my head: I wanted to stay in Como. Jacky would have wanted me to stay. That was a good dream I didn't want to let go of. My family and Jacky's family thought I should return to Britain, to be with the people I knew well, people who cared about me. I knew that was not right. That felt like I was running away. I had to return and do things my own way.

So, two weeks after Jacky was buried, I went straight back to Como and back to work. I worked hard. I often worked all day and then stayed at the office late. Sometimes I took my work home in the evening. I even took over some of Jacky's work to help the company and to fill up more of my empty time.

At weekends I drove somewhere in the mountains and skied all day until I was exhausted. People were kind. I got lots of invitations from the people I worked with, but I didn't accept many of them. I went on short holidays alone, holidays that I had already planned with Jacky . . .

I suppose the friendship with Sandra started in February. Sandra had worked in Jacky's team. She didn't look a lot like Jacky, but . . . perhaps I was just lonely. I knew her well enough to say 'Ciao' in the office and I'd gone out with the team for a pizza before the Christmas holidays. Once or twice I'd found myself looking at her. Once she'd seen me and given me a smile in return.

But I wanted to be alone with my memories of Jacky. One night in January I was walking home from work and met Sandra. We talked as we walked along the winter streets. And when we said goodbye ten minutes later – a warm handshake in the cold evening – I realised that my heart was beating faster than usual and my face was hot. I felt like a boy out on his first date!

Then I forgot all about Sandra again. In February I took over Jacky's marketing team. At our first meeting, when I walked into the room, there was Sandra, sitting right in front of me. I almost couldn't speak at first.

Sandra was very helpful during the meeting – the kind of person all managers need when they're new to a group. And at the end of the meeting she stayed behind when the others had gone. She came up to me.

'Paul,' she said, 'I wanted to tell you how very sorry I am about Jacky.' And then she did a surprising thing. She kissed me lightly on my cheek and was gone, leaving me with the smell of her perfume and the feel of her soft lips on my skin. I felt very confused.

That night at home I cried for the first time since Jacky's death. I cried for hours, thinking about my whole life with her, all the good moments, and the emptiness I knew I'd really been trying to cover up. I have never cried as much before or since. For her. For us. For our dream. For me . . . Then I realised that I couldn't continue living and working and going on holiday as though Jacky was still alive. When I went into the bathroom the next morning, and looked at my red eyes and my white face, I thought that it was the start of my new life after Jacky's death.

And it was Sandra who had helped me with that. Yes, in the end, I could say Sandra helped me. Despite everything that happened with me and Sandra, she helped me at that time. That kiss after the meeting had changed something inside me. And change was what I needed after losing Jacky.

I spoke to Sandra after the next meeting, and we walked part of the way through the town together, talking. It became something I looked forward to. I prepared for those group meetings especially well and my new team worked hard. And I knew that at the end of each afternoon meeting I would have a few minutes' walk with Sandra.

At Easter I went on a tour of the villas of Veneto, a tour I had planned with Jacky and I went alone. I often thought of Jacky, of how she would have enjoyed it, but I also thought of Sandra. I sent Sandra a postcard from Veneto. I'd only found out her address because I wanted to see where she lived in Como. But in the darkness of those cheap hotels on my own, after a day of looking at brilliant architecture, I often found myself thinking of her. I pictured her in the office – the smile on her full lips, the dark brown eyes and shoulder-length dark brown hair. In my mind I replayed her light kiss again and again like a film. And I realised I was beginning to wonder what it would be like to kiss her properly, to hold her, to make love with her.

I have to say that I felt guilty about those thoughts. After all it was only four months since Jacky had died.

But I couldn't stop thinking about Sandra. So I sent her a postcard, and signed it, *Love, Paul.*

Chapter 4   *A weekend in the country*

And then in late April, after another of our team meetings, on our now usual walk through town together, she suddenly asked, 'Paul, what are you doing next weekend?'

'Nothing special,' I replied. 'Why?'

'Would you like to come to my family's old house in Magreglio, up in the mountains? It would be good for you to get out of Como.'

I replied at once. 'I'd love to.' I was quite surprised to hear myself answer so quickly. But I was even more surprised when she put her hands on the sides of my face and kissed me on my mouth. I didn't really kiss back, at first, but then I put my arms around her waist and it turned into a long, deep kiss. And it felt so good. Like something I'd always been waiting for. So warm and full. So exciting. Like eating a strange new fruit.

I then walked her all the way home for the first time, stopping for several more kisses on the way, and making plans for the weekend.

Back in my flat I felt as if I was walking on air. Feelings of guilt and excitement mixed – as if I was having a relationship and my wife didn't know. I couldn't sleep. It was a beautiful night, so I took a bottle of white wine out of the fridge and sat on the balcony. I drank the wine and watched the moon rise over the mountains . . . A new life was opening up.

It was pouring with rain when Sandra arrived in her car at nine o'clock on Saturday morning, as arranged. I was ready and ran out of the flat entrance into her car, and into a long kiss. I was so excited that I hardly noticed that the car was a very expensive Alfa Romeo – far bigger than she could have afforded on her salary at Corvo Pharmaceuticals.

There was some kind of electricity between us in the car as we drove along the lakeside road, with heavy rain hiding both the lake and mountains. It made the world inside the car even stranger and more cut off from everything else. I asked her about the house we were going to – she'd not said much when we'd made the arrangements, just that it would be cold at night and to bring warm clothes and walking boots. It had, she said, belonged to her great-grandparents first. Her parents had lived there when they were first married, but now it was just a place to escape to at weekends.

She and her brother had stopped going there much in the last few years. They'd wanted to travel and see other places. Como and Magreglio were not all there was. She laughed. I loved her laugh, so natural and free. An hour later we were there, parking the car under the trees and walking up the wet path past the vegetable garden, in the rain, up to the house. It was very dark inside.

'Where are your parents?' I asked.

'In Como,' she replied. 'Why?'

'Well, I thought they'd be here, doing weekend gardening and things,' I answered, still rather surprised. The old family house, she'd said, and I'd thought the family would be there.

She turned round, very slowly, and walked over to stand

in front of me, her eyes almost black in the low light, but shining, and said, 'Why would I have wanted to bring you if they were here?'

I said something stupid like, 'Oh, I see,' and tried to put my arms around her. She pushed me off, playfully.

'Later,' she said. 'Let's make this place warm first.'

And for the next hour she was busy turning on the heaters in all the rooms while I made a wood fire in the living room. Then we put the food we'd brought in the fridge, and she made coffee. We sat on the sofa drinking it as the fire grew bigger. It was half past eleven.

'Let me show you round now,' she said, and took me on a tour of the house. There was a big living room, a kitchen-dining room, and a modern bathroom downstairs, and three small bedrooms under the roof upstairs.

'This was my bedroom when I was a little girl,' she said in the smallest upstairs room. 'I used to lie here and watch the sun come up over that mountain every morning in summer . . . and look, the sun's coming out now! Let me show you the garden.'

We put our boots on because it was still very wet on the ground outside. We walked hand-in-hand as she showed me where her grandparents had kept chickens, what vegetables her parents were growing this year, the apple tree where she'd played as a girl.

'What's down there?' I asked, pointing to some stone steps going down to a brown door in the side of the house.

'Oh, nothing now,' she said. 'It was where they used to put wine and vegetables sometimes.'

I was just turning away when I noticed the lock on the door – it was new.

'But Sandra . . .' I started. She was already walking back to the house saying something about lunch. She put together one of those delicious simple meals Italians can always make in no time, and we ate it with the good red wine I had brought . . . for her parents! She disappeared while I put more wood on the dying fire. I looked out of the window. The rain was pouring down again. I had hoped we would go for a walk to the village after lunch, but I didn't feel like it in that rain.

'It's raining again, Sandra,' I called. 'What shall we do this afternoon?'

There was no answer. I went into the kitchen – she wasn't there. I thought she'd probably gone to the bathroom, so I went back into the warm living room.

'Paul,' I heard. 'Paul, can you just come up here a moment?' I climbed the stairs wondering what the problem was. The largest bedroom door was open, so I went inside. 'What did you want . . . ?' Sandra was lying on the bed, smiling.

'I thought this might be a good place to spend a wet Saturday afternoon,' she said.

'Well, it looks more fun than the village in the rain,' I managed to say.

Looking back now, it was perhaps the most enjoyable weekend I've ever had. And I've had a few relationships since then. We never did see Magreglio that weekend, nor much of the rest of the house, except for trips to get food or wine from the kitchen!

When I got back to the flat in Como on the Sunday night, I felt deeply physically tired and very happy in a completely new way. Not that I wanted to compare Jacky, but being with Sandra was like a new, adult adventure rather than the more innocent love I'd known before with Jacky.

Chapter 5 *Mystery in Switzerland*

'Let's go to Lugano this afternoon,' said Sandra suddenly. We were just finishing lunch one late June Saturday. Since our trip to Magreglio we'd spent several weekends and many evenings and nights together, mostly in my flat. She still lived with her parents in Como.

'What?' I asked in surprise. Usually, in the afternoons, we would drive to Belaggio to eat cakes, or to Villa Carlotta for a walk in the gardens. 'Why should we go to Switzerland?'

'For a change,' she replied. 'Have you ever been? It's not far, you know.'

'I know. Jacky and I went last November.' By then I could talk about Jacky as if our marriage had finished years ago, not just months ago. Sandra had changed everything.

'And you can drive us in your car, too,' she said.

'OK,' I agreed, happy for the opportunity of driving – she usually drove us everywhere, saying that she knew the roads better. And her Alfa Romeo was much nicer.

'Let's take your car,' I said.

'It's not working at the moment,' she said. I didn't think then she had a reason to use my car to drive to Switzerland. It was only later that I understood.

'But take me home first,' she went on. 'I need to get something.'

After driving up to Belaggio, we took the ferry over Lake

Como to Menaggio then up over the hill and down to Lake Lugano. Next we went along the lakeside road to the customs. There the Italian officers let us straight through the border, but the Swiss officers checked our passports and asked us where we were going. We then continued round to Lugano and parked the car.

We kissed and then walked along to one of the extremely tidy cafés in the square. We ordered two of the large bowls of fruit, ice-cream and cream which the Swiss like so much.

After a few moments, Sandra looked around the square, looked at her watch and then stood up. 'Toilet,' she said and disappeared inside the café. The ice-creams arrived and I started eating mine, wondering why Sandra was taking so long. After five minutes I stood up to see where she was. I couldn't see her inside the café. So for some reason I looked over the pots of flowers and into the part of the square behind where we were sitting . . . and there was Sandra, about a hundred metres away.

She was talking seriously to a very well-dressed man with a bald head and designer sunglasses, who was standing next to a silver Mercedes. The man was obviously quite angry. I saw Sandra open her bag and give him a small package. She then said something else, then turned to walk back to our café.

I sat down again and ate some ice-cream. My heart was beating fast and I wondered what was going on. The surprise trip to Lugano, using my car, meeting the rich man, the package . . . it was like something out of a spy film! I didn't know if I should ask Sandra about it or not.

'Sorry, Paul,' she said when she got back to the table,

giving me a kiss on the cheek. 'There was a queue, and then I took too long doing my make-up.'

'Eat your ice-cream. It's melting,' I heard myself say. Apparently I had decided to be cool and try to find out what was happening later on.

Chapter 6 *The summer holidays*

During the summer in Italy, everything seems to slow down. Most people go on holiday to the beach or the mountains. I hadn't really thought about what to do in the holidays. Jacky and I had talked about driving around southern Italy by car, and although I still liked the idea, I didn't want to do it alone.

It was Sandra who mentioned the subject of holidays, about one week after the Lugano trip. We were in bed in my flat in Como when she turned to me with a serious face and said, 'What are you doing this summer, Paul?'

'I haven't really thought about it,' I answered truthfully. 'What are you doing?'

'Well, I usually spend the first two weeks at our family place at the seaside. It's in Portofino. Have you ever been there?'

'No,' I replied, 'But I've seen some pictures. It's very beautiful.'

'Would you like to come down?' she asked.

'Well . . . er . . . yes. That would be lovely. But . . . er . . . where would I stay?'

'Oh, there's plenty of space,' she answered. 'We'll find you a bed.'

'We?' I asked.

'Oh, yes. All the family will be there, this time,' she said, and added, 'Not like at Magreglio!'

'Oh, I see,' I replied, feeling a little disappointed. But I said yes. Of course I said yes. Why would I say no? She was beautiful and I was in a beautiful country. If I had known what was going to happen I would have said no. Definitely.

Sandra left for Portofino a few days before me. I decided I would visit a few places on my drive down from Como to Portofino. I visited Florence, Lucca and Pisa in Tuscany, before driving north along the coast until I got to Portofino. The narrow roads were heavy with summer traffic, but the scenery was beautiful – green hills covered in trees going straight down into the blue waters of the Mediterranean Sea.

The place itself had once been a fishing village, and there was a group of red and yellow buildings along the sea, with a castle on the other side. The water was full of boats, many of which were luxury yachts. It was wonderful in the strong summer afternoon light.

I couldn't wait to see Sandra. I hadn't seen her in over a week and I was rather surprised to find just how much I was missing her. I realised how important she had become to me since Jacky's death.

And also I still didn't understand her. That locked room at Magreglio, the expensive car she drove, the trip to Lugano and the mysterious meeting and the package; the fact that she'd never told me about her life outside work. (She'd once said that there was a 'family business' which was 'import-export' and that she sometimes helped.)

There was something else that I really only thought about as I was driving down through Italy: why couldn't she see me on two or three occasions? She had said something about 'having to go away somewhere' without explaining anything. I didn't ask too many questions though. It never seemed the right place or the right time. I also felt that if I asked too many questions – about the Lugano package, for example – that she would stop our relationship, and I'd be alone again. And I wasn't sure I wanted to be alone again just now. I also hoped I might find some answers to these questions when I got to Portofino . . .

I eventually found the right road. It was almost at the top of the hill. Number 19, Via Cadorna – the Villa Bellavista. It had a wonderful view over the sea to the castle. I imagined that her family had a flat in the large building, presumably once the holiday home of some rich businessman. Sandra's shining Alfa Romeo, a couple of Mercedes and a bright yellow Fiat sports car were in a parking area next to a large garden. Quite a place!

I parked my dirty old British Metro next to Sandra's car and got out. At the door I couldn't find any surnames to show me which flat was which, so I rang the only bell I could find. The door was answered by a middle-aged woman dressed as a housekeeper.

'Yes?' she asked coldly, looking me up and down.

'Does Sandra Rovello live here?' I asked.

'Miss Alessandra is out. Who shall I say called?' she replied.

'Well, my name's Paul. Paul Morris, and Sandra is . . .' I didn't have to find the right words because there was the noise of a car turning into the drive which made us both turn. My mouth fell open when I realised that it was Sandra, sitting in the silver Mercedes with the man I'd seen her meet in Lugano.

Sandra looked at my dirty car, then across to where I was standing with the housekeeper, and her face was very serious. I walked over to her as she got out of the car.

'Oh, Paul,' she said, smiling weakly. 'How nice. Look, Andrea – here's Paul Morris, my new manager at Corvo. Paul, please meet Andrea Carta.'

It was a difficult situation. I tried to be polite, but I was quite embarrassed as I shook his hand. Andrea just looked at me in an uninterested way.

'I'm going inside, Alessandra,' he said. 'I'll see you later. Goodbye, Mr Morris. Nice to have met you.'

I stood in the lovely garden, in front of the fine villa, with a beautiful young Italian woman, and I had no idea what to think, what to say or what to do. I stared at the ground.

'Paul,' Sandra said when Andrea had gone in, 'let's walk in the garden.' I couldn't say anything. She came and took my hand.

'Come and tell me all about your holidays,' she said. 'What did you visit?'

I didn't really want to, but I walked into the back garden with her and we sat on a seat near a pool full of fish. I felt like one of them, going round and round in circles without understanding where I was.

'Paul,' she said, trying to take my hand, 'why are you so upset?'

'Well, how else should I feel? You invited me here, and

then you . . . you . . . you come driving in with another man,' I replied.

'But there's nothing between us, Paul,' she said. 'He's just a friend of the family. Nothing more.' I turned and looked into her eyes.

'Sandra, I saw you meet him in Lugano,' I said simply.

'Oh . . . he's . . . er . . .' she started.

'Just forget it, Sandra,' I said quietly, and tried to stand up. She pulled me back onto the bench.

'My father just wanted me to give him something,' she said. 'They do business sometimes, Paul. Honestly! Nothing more,' she said.

'Really?' I asked suspiciously.

'Really,' she answered. And then she kissed me. I realise now that she probably kissed me to shut me up, so she wouldn't have to explain anything else. But then I suppose I was feeling so strange about everything – my life – that I kissed her back, long and hard.

'I'm sorry, Paul,' she said again.

'Well, I'd better go. Your father's friend obviously didn't want me around.'

'No, you can't. You must stay now you've come. Don't worry about him. He's just like that. Come on,' she said, taking my hand. 'Let's go and get your things and find you a room.'

Chapter 7   *Getting in deeper*

At eight thirty that evening I came down from my room for pre-dinner drinks with Sandra's parents. Andrea and two other men were introduced as old business partners of her father. There were also two big men, who looked like bodyguards, but they were introduced as workers in the family business. Everyone was very polite and I thanked them for inviting me to stay.

'Oh, don't mention it,' said Mrs Rovello, who was covered in gold jewellery. 'We're so pleased that you could come and visit us. Sandra has been saying wonderful things about you. She has often told us how helpful you have been with her business studies.'

I smiled and thanked her and then looked across at Sandra. Business studies! What had she been telling them? She looked so innocent and calm. She smiled to me and then refilled my glass. Dinner was long and the food was excellent, with local fish as the main course. After dinner Mr Rovello said he had things to talk over, and took the other men into another room, saying, 'Help yourself to drinks, watch TV,' as he closed the door.

Sandra's mother disappeared, and Sandra and I were left alone. I poured myself a very large whisky from one of the bottles on the sideboard, and, taking a mouthful, said, 'So, what's going on? Shall we talk about all this?'

Sandra came up to me and gave me a small kiss on my

cheek. I sat down. I understood nothing. I looked around the room. Expensive antique furniture, a painting by Giorgio Morandi on the wall, Murano glass ... The Rovellos were seriously rich.

'In the morning,' she said. She took my hand and led me upstairs to my bedroom. At the door she said, 'Different rooms, I'm afraid. I'm tired now. Goodnight.' Then she kissed me quickly and she was gone.

In my room I sat down and drank my whisky. There was a TV in the room and I turned it on and looked through the channels – there were the usual Saturday night programmes – game-shows and old films, none of which I was interested in. I kept thinking of Sandra in another room, getting undressed, getting into bed, and of how much I wanted her.

I knew I couldn't sleep immediately, so I decided to get a breath of fresh air. I went downstairs very quietly and out a side door, leaving it open so that I could get back in.

The garden was still warm from the sun and smelt lovely. It was a beautiful night. I walked round the house and suddenly found myself below a room with open windows. I could hear voices coming from inside.

'. . . And that's why she invited him here . . .' Andrea was saying.

'Yes, but it's very dangerous in this situation,' Mr Rovello was saying.

'Oh, no. I don't think so,' said Andrea. 'He obviously doesn't know about anything. Look how easy the Lugano job was. It was a very clever idea.'

'Well, we were still lucky,' argued Mr Rovello.

'But do you think Sandra will be able to persuade him

to go to England?' asked one of the business partners.

'I think he'll do anything she asks him,' replied Andrea.

I couldn't believe what I was hearing. I listened hard to catch every word.

'Good, because if we can get our things through to London quickly, now that Andrea's American connection has been closed down, it might help us to keep our hands on that market . . .' said one of the partners.

'But he must know nothing,' said Andrea. 'Alessandra needs to . . .'

That was the last thing I heard of their conversation, but I didn't know that until I woke up in my room an hour or so later. I was lying in bed. Sandra was sitting beside me. I had a wet towel on my head and a terrible headache.

'You're going to have to rest for a while,' she said. 'Stupid boy!'

I couldn't see very clearly. 'What happened?' I asked.

'Oh, poor Paul. What were you doing outside the house in the dark? One of the bodyguards thought you were a burglar. He didn't realise you were a guest of the family.'

'Well, there was no need for him to hit me,' I said, gently touching my head.

'I know. I'm sorry. The guards are not very gentle, I'm afraid. But now, Paul, you've got to get some sleep,' said Sandra, putting down the towel and drying her hands.

'But Sandra . . .' I started.

'Not now, Paul,' she replied. 'Go to sleep and we'll talk about it in the morning.'

And she kissed me on the top of my head and went, leaving me in the dark room with a headache, and more questions than when I'd arrived at Villa Bellavista a few hours earlier.

As I lay there, I turned everything around in my head. I was very frightened. I felt like an animal that has been caught. What did these people want from me? Should I get up and leave now? How could I get out of this horrible situation? Damn Sandra! Damn Jacky! Damn that roof-tile! My angry thoughts brought me back to reality. I couldn't blame my dead wife. This was my fault. I had been so interested in Sandra, I had needed her so much after Jacky's death that I hadn't thought clearly about anything. Eventually, I fell asleep.

Chapter 8   *Preparations*

I woke early. It was about four o'clock. I needed some air, so I went onto the balcony outside my room. It was still dark, but I could hear the sea. I looked across to the castle which had lights shining on it. The wind was playing with the trees. It was very beautiful. As I stood there, I heard a noise below me. I looked down. I was just in time to see one of the bodyguards standing close to my car. Unfortunately it was still quite dark in the car park, so I couldn't see exactly what he was doing. But it didn't make me very happy.

From what I'd heard about 'the American connection' and 'getting things through to London' I thought I had finally found out what the 'family business' was: selling drugs or something else illegal. And when I put what I'd heard this evening together with what I'd seen before – the locked room at Magreglio, the package in Lugano – it appeared quite clear now. Why hadn't I thought about it before? Why hadn't I said anything in Lugano? I thought how stupid I'd been to let myself get into this mess. And now I also understood something else.

It seemed that Sandra had been using me all along. She had already used me once to take something – drugs, perhaps, or gold – to Lugano. And in my car. Just imagine if we'd been caught! And she had only invited me here because she wanted to persuade me to go with her to

England with something else – something that was even more important. How stupid I had been!

I went back into my room, and after lying, thinking about all of the strange things I had seen and heard, I finally went to sleep again. At about ten o'clock I was woken by Sandra with some coffee and rolls.

'Hello,' she said brightly, as she opened the curtains. 'How do you feel this morning?'

'OK, I suppose,' I replied, feeling my head carefully.

'Well, here's some nice breakfast for you,' she said, smiling. 'When you're ready come and find me in the garden by the pool. I've got something I want to talk about.'

'Sandra . . .' I started, but she had already gone. So I had my breakfast, got myself ready and went down into the heat of the Mediterranean garden to find Sandra. When she saw me coming, she got up and came towards me.

'Hello, Paul,' she said, taking my hand. 'You look much better. I'm so sorry about last night.'

'Are you?' I replied suspiciously. We sat on the seat by the pool again, and she kissed my cheek. I felt very uncertain about what to do and say after everything that had happened.

'Of course I am,' she said. 'How are you feeling now?'

'OK,' I said. She kissed me again.

'Good. Because I've just had a great idea. We've got a lot of time before we have to go back to work in Como. Why don't we go to England?'

'Why should we?' I asked simply. I wondered what she would answer after what I had heard last night. And I also wondered exactly what she knew about the 'family business'.

'You could show me everything. We could have a little holiday together in England. What do you say?'

I thought for a long time before I spoke.

'I would like to go to England with you Sandra. Very much. I enjoy being with you, and you're really the only friend I've got. But I need the answers to one or two questions before we go.'

'What questions, Paul?' she asked.

'I need to know about Andrea, about what happened in Lugano, about what I heard last night,' I said. 'And I need some honest answers.'

'I've told you about Andrea,' Sandra said. 'He's simply one of my father's business partners. He manages our exports to the USA, but there have been some problems there recently. That's why he's here talking to my father this weekend.'

'So why did we go to Lugano that time?' I asked.

'For an afternoon out,' she said, 'and because my father asked me to meet Andrea and give him something he'd forgotten.'

'What was it?' I asked, staring at her hard. She stared back.

'I don't know, Paul,' she answered. 'Papers, or something. I work for Corvo Pharmaceuticals, not my father's business. It was nothing to do with me. I was just doing something for my father.'

She seemed to be telling the truth. Maybe I was just imagining everything. Perhaps I had watched too many James Bond films when I was younger!

Or perhaps I just wanted to believe her. I looked at her. She was very beautiful. I found it very difficult to see her as a criminal. Perhaps they had just been talking about normal business last night, but then why did the guard hit me?

'Yes, but why did that guard hit me last night?' I asked.

'I told you,' Sandra replied. 'He thought you were a burglar. They get very nervous. It looked suspicious. Anyway, how is your poor head now?'

She reached up and turned my head to look at the place where I'd been hit. Then she turned my face towards her and kissed me.

'It looks much better now,' she said. 'So, shall we go to England or not?'

I took a deep breath.

'All right,' I said.

'Good. Let's go tomorrow,' she said. 'I want to get away from here as soon as possible!'

Chapter 9 *Into France*

By ten o'clock the next morning we were already driving along the motorway west of Genoa, nearing the French border. Light shone off the sea and onto the surrounding hills. The journey had been easy so far. When we got to the border itself, however, we met unexpected queues of slowly moving traffic. As we came up to the customs buildings there were policemen everywhere wearing special clothes and carrying sub-machine guns.

My heart jumped. Perhaps I was involved in something illegal after all! Perhaps I was going to be caught and finish in prison! I looked at Sandra. She was chewing her lip and looking nervous.

But the police just waved us through. Obviously they were looking for someone else. Sandra looked much less worried when the cars began to increase speed on the French side of the border. I was starting to feel suspicious again. Her behaviour had not been normal for someone who was just on holiday with her boyfriend. Perhaps we were carrying something in the car after all.

'Sandra,' I said, 'are you sure we're not doing something illegal?'

'Why?' she asked. 'What do you mean?'

'Well, it's just that you looked so nervous at the border back there with the police . . .'

'Oh, please, Paul!' she said. 'I'm tired of all your questions. Don't be so suspicious.' She wasn't so sweet to me now.

After that we didn't speak for a long time. The motorway was quite busy as we drove near the famous tourist resorts of Cannes and Nice, and through the red Provençal countryside. By three o'clock I was feeling tired, hungry and needed to go to the toilet. 'What shall we do about stopping?' I asked.

'Let's stop at the next service station,' she said. 'I need to get out of the car, too.' At the service station, I first filled the car with petrol, then went and parked the car in front of the shop. I went to the toilet. I was just washing my hands when a cleaner came in through another door, with a cheerful *'Bonjour, monsieur'*.

For some reason I looked out of the open door. It was at the back of the building. As I looked, a silver Mercedes drove along the road from the car park. I was sure it was Andrea's car, although I couldn't see the number plate or the driver.

I went into the shop. When I looked through the big window I could see Sandra standing next to our car. She was talking fast Italian to someone on her mobile phone. I bought some orange juice and mineral water and went out to where the car was standing. Sandra was waiting by the car.

'Who were you talking to?' I asked.

She looked annoyed. Didn't she want me to know that she had been talking to someone?

'What's the matter with you, Paul?' she asked. 'You are

suspicious of everything and everyone. I was just talking to my father, actually, to tell him that I was all right. He worries about me.'

'I see,' I said. But now I didn't really believe her, I couldn't believe her now, not after I thought I'd seen Andrea's Mercedes.

We drove on all afternoon. She was angry with me, but even that made me suspicious: why should she be angry if she had nothing to hide? She had the map-book open on her knees. Our only conversations were about directions and roads. Sandra's mobile phone rang three times and she answered in monosyllables – '*Sì*' and '*No*' and '*Ciao*' – which told me nothing.

I kept looking ahead and in my mirror to see if Andrea's silver car was anywhere, but it never was. But as time went on I did have an idea that we were being followed, at a distance. There was a yellow Fiat sports car that I often noticed several cars behind us. It could go much faster than my little Metro, and I couldn't understand why it just sat there behind us. And then I remembered that there had been a yellow Fiat exactly like that one in the car park when I had arrived at the Portofino villa.

On and on we went in the hot French summer sun. The red southern earth turned into rock and then into greener hill country, and as darkness fell we were getting near Clermont-Ferrand.

'I'm getting tired,' I said, breaking a long, long silence in which I'd had nothing but my own thoughts to play with. 'And hungry.'

'OK,' said Sandra. 'Let's find somewhere for the night.'

Chapter 10 *An unhappy drive*

Half an hour later I was parking the car in front of the Hotel de la Poste in the village of Issoire. I got out of the car and looked around. I couldn't see the silver Mercedes or the yellow Fiat. But that didn't mean anything. Inside, Sandra checked us in with the hotel receptionist in excellent French, and we went upstairs to our second-floor room.

'I'm just going out for a minute,' said Sandra. She left immediately. I lay down on the bed, feeling too tired to ask why and where. Half an hour later she reappeared. 'Right,' she said brightly. 'It's time for dinner. I've found a lovely little restaurant just across the square, and I've booked us a table for half an hour's time. Are you still hungry?'

'I could eat a horse!' I said, standing up. I walked to where she was and put my arms round her.

'Let's be friends, Sandra. I hate these long silences between us.'

'I want to be friends,' she said. 'But you keep saying terrible things about me . . .'

'I'm sorry,' I said. 'But you must see how difficult it is for me to understand what's happening.'

'There's really nothing to understand, Paul,' she answered simply. 'Let's just enjoy our holiday.'

We kissed. A long deep kiss. Our first that day. It felt very good. I couldn't help myself.

After a very good dinner in the restaurant, I had a long shower and then fell into bed. I was very tired after my day of driving and I was asleep as soon as my head touched the pillow. I had the feeling that Sandra left the room and came back while I was asleep, but I have no idea what she did.

*   *   *

At six thirty the next morning Sandra, already fully dressed and made-up, woke me.

'There's *café au lait* and croissants on the table over there,' she said in a cold voice. 'I'd like to leave at seven if that's all right with you.'

Then she went out again. I got out of bed with difficulty. My body hurt after driving the day before. I had a quick cool shower to wake myself up. I dressed and while I was drinking coffee and eating a croissant Sandra kept walking into the room, looking out of the window, then walking out again.

Looking out of the window down onto the square a few minutes later, I was just in time to see a silver Mercedes with Swiss number plates turn the corner and drive out of view. So Andrea really was around, I thought. Once again.

I wondered how I was going find out what was happening – it was difficult to ask Sandra directly. I looked around the room to check that I'd left nothing behind and suddenly noticed Sandra's mobile telephone lying next to her coat on the chair.

I had an idea. I picked up the phone, went into the bathroom and dropped it inside the toilet. Then I heard the door open. I washed my hands, and walked back into the bedroom. Perhaps it was a silly thing to do, but I was fed up with her talking on the mobile phone.

'Your driver is ready, madam,' I said to Sandra, trying to make a joke. I picked up the two cases. She laughed – which was lovely to hear – and we left the hotel.

We drove out of the village with its dark stone buildings, past the pretty church which I'd visited with Jacky. That seemed such a long time ago now. We stopped for petrol on the edge of the village and soon were back on the E11 motorway driving north.

We had passed Clermont-Ferrand and were getting close to Bourges. Nothing had happened. The traffic was normal. I drove easily. The weather was cloudy but dry, and there was no sign of the other two cars. And Sandra had not yet noticed that her mobile phone was missing. We said nothing of importance. I sometimes asked for water from the bottles which she had bought in the morning. She also gave me apples and chocolate at regular intervals.

As I drove I thought about everything that had happened on the journey so far. Sandra's nervousness at the French border, the two cars that seemed to be following us, the way that Sandra went out of the hotel room several times, the phone-calls she kept receiving . . .

I knew I had to find out what was really going on quickly, before we got to England. I felt happy that the mobile phone had now gone. That made it difficult for Sandra to call Andrea or anyone, and gave me more of a chance of finding out the truth.

Suddenly there was a scream. Sandra was pulling things out of her handbag, turning to search the pockets of her coat on the back seat, looking through the maps in the door pocket and feeling under her seat.

'Shit!' she shouted, and banged her hands on the map on her knee.

'What's the matter?' I asked, trying to sound worried and innocent at the same time.

'I can't find my phone,' she screamed, searching violently in her bag again.

'Calm down,' I said. 'It must be somewhere around. Take your time and have a good look.'

She tried again, but (of course!) it was useless.

'I don't suppose you know anything about it, do you?' she asked, turning to look at me.

'It's your phone, Sandra. You always have it with you. I haven't seen it,' I replied.

She put the things back into her handbag, crossed her arms across her chest and stared, hard-faced, at the endless motorway in front of her.

Chapter 11 *A story is told*

At around one o'clock we reached Paris. Sandra didn't want to go through the city, so we drove around the eastern side of the capital. I was starting to make a plan in my head. I realised I had more chance of finding out what was happening on the ordinary roads we were now using than on the motorway. There were traffic lights, people and police stations. Something would happen to help me. If a chance roof-tile could put me into this situation then something else unlikely could happen to get me out of it.

Why did I believe that some unexpected opportunity would arrive to help me? I have no idea. But it did. The cloudy sky, which had been getting darker the further north we got, turned to rain. At first the rain was light, but soon it was heavy enough for me to slow the car right down. I put the windscreen wipers at double speed and water from heavy lorries, driving out of Paris, was pushed hard against my small car.

And soon it became so dark, with thunder and lightning all around us, that I was driving along at less than twenty kilometres per hour.

Through the rain my headlights lit up a sign for a cross-roads with the names of several small villages on it. I knew that soon we would be back onto main roads. I had to do something now. I thought that it would be difficult for Andrea and the others to follow us along small country lanes, so I decided to take a chance.

I checked behind me for headlights. There were some in the distance. I could see no more than fifty metres ahead. As we got closer to the crossroads I suddenly turned the steering wheel and drove quickly across the road and down a country lane. There was a loud sound of a horn and flashing of lights as a big lorry went past just behind us, but I'd done it. Sandra was thrown around by the violent and unexpected turn.

'Are you mad?' she screamed when she recovered. 'You nearly got us killed! Get back onto the other road at once!'

'No,' I said very calmly and quietly.

'Get back this minute!' she shouted. 'Or I'll . . . Or I'll . . .'

'Or you'll what?' I asked. There was no answer. It was still pouring with rain. I drove the car for a few kilometres to make sure no-one was following us. Then I stopped the car by the side of the road. I had no idea what to do next. The only thought I had was that Sandra must have planned a meeting with Andrea for that evening.

I thought that Sandra's 'friends' would now be worried and suspicious because they hadn't been able to talk to her on her mobile phone. And they would almost certainly be very angry. But I suddenly realised that if there was something in my car that Andrea and Mr Rovello wanted to get to England, I was the key to the success of the operation. For some reason none of them could make the trip to England themselves – they needed someone else to do it. Perhaps they already had criminal records.

'So,' said Sandra once we had stopped moving, 'What are we going to do now?'

'You think about it,' I said, and pushing the seat back, I

closed my eyes. Soon I could hear the sound of Sandra crying. At first I tried to ignore her but then I couldn't stand it any more. I turned to her.

'Sandra, what's the matter?' I asked, touching her arm. She pushed me off.

'Leave me alone. You've caused nothing but problems all along.'

It was difficult to understand her through the hand that covered her face and through the tears.

'Hey, come on!' I replied. 'It's you who's behaving strangely, not me.'

At this she started crying even more.

'It's not me,' she said with difficulty. 'They make me do these things.'

'What do you mean?' I asked, totally confused by what she had just said and wanting to hear more. Slowly she tried to stop crying. She blew her nose. She looked a mess. Her eyes and face were red and her make-up was in black lines around her cheeks. She looked like a little lost girl and I suddenly felt very sorry for her.

'Can you tell me?' I asked very gently, reaching for her hand and holding it to give her strength.

In a very quiet voice she started to talk.

'It's very difficult to explain, Paul, but you know some things already, and I want to show you that I didn't want to do any of this. It's him.'

'It's who?' I asked.

'Andrea,' she answered, starting to cry again. As soon as she was able to, she continued.

'My father was a successful businessman. He had a small company with those two other men you saw in Portofino as partners. They were involved in the import and export of reproduction furniture, furniture that looks like antiques. They had business connections all over the world, but especially in England and France. It was a good business for a long time, but about ten years ago, things started to get difficult.'

'But where does Andrea come in?' I asked, taking hold of her hand again.

'Business was so slow that my father and his partners owed a lot of money and they thought they might have to close their business down. Then they met Andrea. He had very good connections in America where the reproduction furniture business was still good. It seemed that Andrea could help the company, so my father and his partners decided to let him try.'

'And were they successful?' I asked.

'Very,' Sandra answered. 'In fact they were so successful that at the end of the first year my father and his partners made Andrea a partner, too. Everyone was happy – it seemed as if everything was going to be all right. Andrea was very sweet to our family at first, and especially to me. And I thought he was very nice.'

'He's a lot older than you, isn't he?' I said.

'Yes, Paul, he is . . . but we started a relationship. My parents were very happy about it. The family is still very important for Italians. They felt that Andrea had saved them. He was part of the business, and some time in the future, they thought, he might be part of the family. Everything would be safe for me. And I loved him . . . At least, I did at first . . .'

She stopped and looked down, a painful expression on

her face. I gave her a light kiss on her cheek, then she went on. 'Soon, however, my father started to get very worried about what was happening in the business. More furniture was going and coming from America than in the first year, but the profits were much bigger. My father couldn't understand it. The new customers seemed to be paying a lot more for the furniture than the companies he had worked with before.

'Of course we all enjoyed the increased profits. We all had the car we wanted. My father bought Villa Bellavista and forgot about Magreglio. My mother was able to fill the house with the glass and paintings she had always wanted. Everyone was happy. On the surface. But underneath my father knew something wasn't right.

'In the end, about two years later, he and the other two partners asked Andrea to explain what was happening, and the truth came out. He started off buying and selling reproduction furniture for the company, but then he started to change the reproduction furniture for real antique chairs and cupboards. These antiques were mostly stolen, but customs authorities thought it was just reproduction furniture. He was taking large amounts of very valuable antique Italian furniture into America. It was very clever, but it was clear that he was just using my father's company. He was also bringing back all kinds of works of art from there.'

'My God!' I shouted. 'But why didn't your father report Andrea to the police?'

'He couldn't,' she replied very simply. 'Don't you see that my father and his partners were in it too. They were the owners of the company, and they had enjoyed the profits of this illegal business. Even I was a small part of it. I had my car, my clothes, my exciting holidays, and my regular trips across the border into Switzerland to take things . . .'

'What things?' I said, wanting to know exactly what I'd had in the car that day.

'Oh, antique jewellery usually – I'd been stopped at the border the time before I asked you to drive to Lugano. Fortunately I'd had nothing on me. But that's why Andrea told me to ask you to take me there in your car. You were not suspicious to the customs authorities, and we needed to get it there quickly. It was for a very important customer.'

'But surely if you'd explained everything to the police they would have understood,' I started.

'Oh, Paul, it's not so simple,' she said loudly. 'Don't you understand that we are all in Andrea's power, even though my father still looks as if he runs the company. All of us would go to prison if anyone had said anything.'

'And so it was Andrea's idea to get me to drive you to England with the . . . the . . . whatever it is we've got in this car?' I asked.

'Well, I really wanted to go there with you on holiday,' she replied, looking at me nervously. 'But something went wrong in the United States two weeks ago and Andrea said we would have to take something with us . . . and, oh Paul, I didn't want to get you involved. I really didn't. You must believe me!'

'Why are they following us now?' I asked.

'They want to make sure that the operation is successful. When we found out the truth about Andrea I finished our relationship, so he doesn't trust me completely.'

I knew now what one of the bodyguards was doing with

my car at four o'clock in the morning at Portofino. I had one more question. 'What is in my car? What have they put in my car?'

'I don't know. Probably paintings that they want to get out of the country.'

I looked at Sandra. I could see she was telling the truth and a warm feeling went through my body.

'Oh, Sandra!' I said softly, putting my arms around her and pulling her close to me. 'I believe you. I thought it was you who had been using me all this time.'

She let me hold her close to me, and I felt her start crying again. I held her quietly for what seemed like a long time. Finally she sat up, cleared her eyes, and looked at me.

'No, Paul. Not at all. Never!' she said. 'I didn't want to get you involved in any of the mess that my family is in. But Andrea says that he will tell the police and my family will all end up in prison because everything is in my father's name.' And here the tears came again, and she cried and cried in my arms.

Chapter 12   *A bad morning*

We sat in that old car of mine on the side of the road and held each other silently for a very long time. Then we started to talk. We decided that the best thing to do would be to return to Italy. We would return to Italy and meet Sandra's father somewhere where Andrea couldn't find us. We would phone Mr. Rovello as soon as we could to explain what had happened and arrange a meeting place. We thought it was best to try and persuade him to go to the Italian police and explain the whole situation. We felt the police would understand the Rovello family's problems. After all, it was Andrea who did the illegal business.

The rain had stopped, but it was getting dark when we stopped in front of a small hotel at Chateaudon, a hundred kilometres south. It had taken us longer to travel back because we had decided to stay off the motorways in case Andrea and his friends were looking for us.

After a shower and change of clothes, we ate the usual excellent French hotel dinner in the restaurant downstairs. It was a quiet meal. We were both very tired, and each of us felt very pleased in our own way. Sandra had told me the truth and didn't have to hide what was happening from me any more. And I finally understood much of the story which I had been involved in. Of course, we were both still worried about the next part. Many difficult problems lay ahead, not least getting back to Italy safely. After a couple of glasses of Calvados in the small bar, we went to bed early. We slept closely together all night, feeling the new warmth of being on the same side.

*   *   *

At about six thirty the next morning we were woken by loud knocking on the bedroom door. Sandra got out of bed with difficulty and went across to the door.

'Wait, Sandra . . .' I shouted, waking up a bit, 'Find out who . . .'

It was too late. At that moment she turned the key and the door opened. Sandra was pushed across the room onto the bed by Andrea. One of the guards I'd seen in Portofino followed him in, locking the door behind him. They were both holding guns.

Sandra moved close to me on the bed, and I put my arm around her. She was shaking with fear and her face was very white. The two men stood at the foot of the bed, staring at us and looking dangerous.

'So,' said Andrea slowly, with a horrible smile on his face, 'we have found our runaway lovers.'

He and the other man looked at each other and laughed.

'But how . . . ?' I started.

'You stupid Englishman!' shouted the big man. 'Do you imagine we would have let you go driving around Europe with a car containing a number of priceless . . .'

'Careful!' cut in Andrea. 'A car containing some very valuable things, without keeping a close check on where you were? We are not stupid, Mr Morris! I put a very strong radio signal on your car in Portofino so that we could always find you. And here you are!' said Andrea, with a cold laugh.

Sandra turned to me with an 'I didn't know anything about it' look on her face, and I took her hand to show that I believed her.

'Now get dressed and packed and be ready in twenty minutes!' ordered Andrea. 'Take out the telephone.'

The big guard pulled the telephone off the wall. Then they both left, locking the bedroom door behind them. I pulled Sandra closer to me, and we held each other for a few moments.

'What shall we do now?' she asked, standing up.

'I have no idea at present,' I answered, still surprised that they'd been able to find us so easily, and angry with myself for not having thought that they would have checked our movements closely. As they said, whatever was in the car was far too valuable ('priceless' was the guard's word) to leave to chance. Once again I wondered what it could be. I got out of bed and walked over to my suitcase.

'Well, I think we'd better do as they ask,' said Sandra. 'We can make a plan as we go along. And Paul . . .'

'Yes?' I turned to face her, and she walked over to where I was standing. 'I really didn't know anything about the radio signal in the car,' she said.

'I know you didn't,' I replied, giving her a smile, and stretching out my hands to her. She took my hands in hers and stood looking at me. 'And anyway, there's something I want to tell you.'

'Yes?' she said with an uncertain look on her face.

'Sandra, I love you,' I said, and then added: 'And when all this is over I want to be with you all the time. I . . . I . . . I want to marry you.'

I must say that I hadn't really thought about marriage,

but I'd realised after her explanation yesterday that I really did love her. I'd been so uncertain about my feelings, confused as they had been at first with Jacky's death and then with this awful nightmare. And now it seemed as if a window had been opened in a dark room, and sunlight was coming in so that I could understand everything.

'Oh, Paul,' she said, staring at me almost in disbelief. 'How can you love me when all I've done is bring you so much trouble? And when we don't even know how we're going to get out of this?'

'I know it looks impossible at present,' I replied, pulling her closer to me, 'but we'll be all right. Just tell me one thing: do you love me?'

'I do, Paul, I do. It just seems so difficult now . . .' She stopped speaking and tears came to her eyes. I put my hands on either side of her face, and looked into her eyes.

'No crying now, my love,' I said softly. 'I need all your help now. OK?'

She nodded, and smiled. I gave her a kiss on her pretty lips.

'Come on,' I said. 'Let's get ready.'

*   *   *

Twenty minutes later we were let out of the room by the guard and taken downstairs to the car park where Andrea was waiting for us. Their cars were parked on either side of mine.

'Now listen very carefully,' Andrea started in an unpleasant voice, pointing at me. 'You've already given us enough problems. And this new delay means that we will have to wait a day or two here in France.'

'Why?' asked Sandra.

'Because our connections in England tell us that the customs authorities at the border will be checking everyone who goes into the country. Apparently, they are looking for some international terrorist group. If we had got in this morning it would have been all right, but now we are too late. Because of your *boyfriend*.'

'So what are we going to do?' I asked.

'We're going to have a little holiday, Mr Morris, at the French seaside,' answered Andrea. 'We are going to drive to Dieppe and wait until you can cross the Channel to Newhaven. It's about 250 kilometres to Dieppe from here. We can easily get there by lunchtime. We will all go together. Alessandra – you will go in my car so you don't get any more clever ideas about running away. Mr Morris – you will follow our guard here. His yellow car is very easy to see, so you will not make any mistakes. Do you understand? After all, you would not like anything to happen to Alessandra, would you?'

'What do you mean?' I asked.

'I don't think I need to explain,' said Andrea, pushing Sandra towards his Mercedes. 'Just do as you have been told and everything will be all right.'

Chapter 13 *The farmhouse*

I did as I was told. I drove along the main roads northwards between the two cars. Whenever I looked in the mirror I could see Sandra sitting beside Andrea in the front seat of the silver Mercedes, as she must have done many times before.

I felt very alone. I had no idea what to do, especially now that I was not with Sandra any more. It seemed to take away my ability to think and act. And anyway, after what Andrea had said, I was afraid of what they might do to her if I tried to escape. So I drove along in a kind of dream.

*   *   *

The towns came and went. The roads were dry, the traffic was not too busy and by half past eleven we were driving into the suburbs of Dieppe. There, the guard signalled and stopped at the roadside; I stopped behind him, and Andrea came up and parked right behind me. The guard and Andrea got out and had a discussion with a map opened on the roof of the guard's car. I turned round and smiled to Sandra, and she blew me a kiss back.

Once the two men had decided where to go, they got back into their cars and we started again. I followed the yellow Fiat sports car into the town centre, then out along a coast road until we came to a lonely old farmhouse near the sea. The guard turned into the drive and then into a car park behind the farmhouse. I followed. Andrea and Sandra drove past the house. I wondered where they had gone to, but soon realised that they had been to collect the keys.

'Right, you,' said the guard, when they had returned, 'get out of the car, get your bags and follow me.' I did as I was told. We were let into the house through the back door by Andrea.

'Car keys,' ordered the big guard, stretching out his hand. I gave them to him.

'Don't forget to take his passport, too,' said Andrea. 'I've already got Alessandra's.'

'Upstairs, both of you,' said the guard.

We were taken upstairs and put in different rooms at the back of the house. The doors were locked.

'Please,' I heard Sandra shouting, 'I need to go to the bathroom, and I'm hungry and thirsty, too.'

'Wait,' came the answer. I could hear Andrea and the guard talking below, but it was impossible to understand what they were saying. Some time later the door opened and closed with a bang, and I heard the yellow Fiat starting. Looking out of the window, I saw it drive off.

It returned about half an hour later, and soon footsteps came up the stairs. Sandra's door was opened and she was allowed to go to the bathroom, before being locked in again. Then it was my turn. Before being locked in again, I was given two large bottles of mineral water, some French bread, some Camembert cheese and two bars of chocolate. I sat down on the bed and ate.

When I'd finished I started to examine the room carefully. It was simply furnished – a bed, a table and chair, a wardrobe and a colourful carpet in the middle. There was one window which looked out onto the car park, the untidy garden behind, and across some fields. The sea was in the opposite direction. I wondered what to do next. I was a prisoner. I needed to escape. But how?

I walked to the window and tried to open it. It was impossible. I walked over to the door. It was quite thick, and well locked. What else could I do? The walls? I put my ear against the wall between my room and Sandra's room, hoping I could hear something. I couldn't. I knocked on the wall and waited. Nothing. I knocked harder and waited. There was an answering knock.

Knock, knock, I went. Knock, knock, she went.

'Hello,' I said. Nothing. Obviously it was a thick wall. There was no way out of the room. Disappointed, I lay down on the bed on my back with my hands behind my head staring up at the ceiling. The ceiling! There in the middle of the ceiling was a door which went up into the roof.

I lay there for a while looking at the small door in the ceiling, wondering how I was going to get up to it. It was about three and a half metres from the floor. I sat up and looked around the room. I moved the chair from under the table, and with no noise I picked up the table itself, and carried it across the room until it was underneath the door in the ceiling. I put the chair next to it and climbed up on the table. The ceiling was just above my head now, and I put my arms up and pushed the painted wooden door. It stayed shut. I pushed again, harder this time, and there was a small movement. I kept pushing.

Suddenly, the door moved upwards with a rather loud

noise. I stood still and listened, hoping that the two men downstairs had heard nothing. As there was no sudden running of feet on the stairs, I guessed I had been lucky. Next I pulled the chair up onto the table and carefully climbed up on it. I pushed the wooden door to one side and put my head and shoulders through the hole and looked into the space below the roof.

I had no idea what to expect, but I was surprised by what I saw. The roof was very high and there were two windows through which sunlight came, lighting the whole central area. There were some boxes at one end, and lots of old farm things. This had probably been a space to keep things when the building was a farmhouse. There was probably a door to the outside somewhere through which things would be pulled up from below.

I looked around carefully. Above the window of my room I could see three lines of light in the wall. They were in the shape of a double door. I was just going to get up into the roof, when I heard a noise from below. Quickly, I put the door back over the opening, but I couldn't make it fall back into place! There was no time now, as the footsteps were at the top of the stairs. I climbed down from the chair and off the table, then put the chair back onto the floor.

I heard a knock on Sandra's door, and the guard's voice asking in Italian if she wanted anything. Sandra said something, the lock was turned and she was allowed to go to the bathroom again.

While this was happening I replaced the table and chair in their positions. As I lay down on the bed, the key was turned in the lock of the door and the big guard walked in.

I looked across at him, hoping he wouldn't look up at the ceiling where there were dirty marks by the door.

'Do you want anything?' he asked roughly.

'Yes, I'd like to go to the bathroom, please.'

I went over to my case and took out my wash-bag and a towel, and walked out to the bathroom. I looked at my face in the mirror. I was a mess. I hadn't shaved in the morning, I had dirt on my face from the roof and lines under my eyes from having little sleep and worrying a lot. I washed and shaved and felt better. The guard was sitting on a chair in the corridor when I came out. As I passed Sandra's room I knocked on the door.

'Sandra,' I shouted. 'Are you all right?'

'Paul,' came her voice. 'Yes, I'm fine. What about you? What's happening?'

'I'm OK,' I replied. 'I don't know what's going on. I suppose we're just waiting until we can cross to England. I don't know if —'

'All right,' said the guard, walking up to me. 'That's enough. Get back in your room.'

I did as I was told. The door was locked behind me again, and the guard's footsteps disappeared downstairs. I looked at my watch – it was five o'clock. I decided not to get up in the roof now. I would wait until Andrea and the guard had gone to bed. I ate some more bread, cheese and chocolate. At ten o'clock there was another visit from the guard to let me go to the bathroom. I said goodnight to Sandra through the door.

Chapter 14 *Escape*

Back in my room, I looked through my case and decided what things I would take with me. I changed into dark clothes so that I would not be seen so easily at night. Then I set my alarm clock for one o'clock in the morning, got into bed fully dressed and switched off the light. It was a good thing I did so. At around midnight, I heard footsteps coming upstairs. My door was unlocked, the light was switched on for a second as either Andrea or the guard checked on me.

After that I lay in the dark waiting. I must have fallen asleep because I woke up suddenly when the alarm went off at one o'clock. I sat up in the dark, listening. It was very quiet. I could hear the noise of the sea outside. I got out of bed and repeated my actions of the afternoon with the table and chair. Then I tied my trainers together, and put them round my neck. I'd be much quieter in just my socks, I thought.

Soon I was pulling myself up into the space under the roof. The floor made a noise as I stood up. Moonlight came in through the windows, giving me a little light. I stood still for a minute letting my eyes get used to things. Then I walked slowly and softly across to the double doors. I couldn't see how they opened in the afternoon. I would have to do it all by touch now in the dark. I found the door, and moved my hands up and down it. There was no lock and key in the middle, so I moved down to the bottom. There was something metal there. I felt and turned it, and pulled upwards. Nothing happened. I put both hands on it and pulled hard up. The door moved suddenly, and I fell over backwards with a noise onto the floor.

I lay there for a minute or two breathing fast after the effort. I listened hard to see if the noise had woken anyone. Silence. I stood up and pushed the door. It swung open with a horrible noise – it must have been shut for years. I waited again.

There was still no sound from inside the house. I looked down. It was, I suppose, about six or seven metres to the ground. I hadn't thought about how I would get down. I walked quietly around, looking to see if I could find a rope or a ladder or something else to help. There was nothing. I went over to the door and looked down again. I suppose I'll have to jump, I thought. But I didn't like the idea of jumping down onto the hard ground.

I put on my trainers, then I sat on the edge of the roof door. It was a long way down! I waited for a moment and then dropped down and then rolled over as I hit the ground. I stood up and brushed myself down. I walked over to my car. The doors and boot were all locked.

I sat down beside the car in the dark. I quickly thought through what I needed to do and made a list in my mind: one, get back into the house; two, find my car keys and, if possible, our passports; three, get Sandra; four, leave. It didn't sound very easy!

I took a deep breath and walked to the back door of the house. To my surprise it was open. I walked in, leaving the door open behind me for a quick escape if necessary. I stood and listened. But I couldn't hear anything. I took my trainers off, putting them round my neck again. It was very dark in the house, and I wondered if I could turn on the light to look for the keys.

Suddenly there was a noise upstairs. A door opened, and I heard footsteps go along the corridor. I stood very still. The bathroom door opened and shut. I moved quickly out of the hall and into the living room where the moonlight through the windows showed me a large sofa. I got down behind it. I heard the toilet, then a light was turned on, and footsteps came down the stairs. I felt cold sweat running down my back as they came closer. The light in the living room was switched on, and someone walked across and went into the kitchen. I heard the outside door shut.

I looked out from behind the sofa, checking the room. Table and chairs, a fireplace, two armchairs, a large clock showing one thirty, a cupboard, a TV, a bookshelf . . . My eyes went back to the cupboard. I thought I could see some keys and papers on it.

At that moment there was a noise from the kitchen, and someone came out. I got down behind the sofa again. The light went off, and the footsteps went back upstairs. I hoped that he wouldn't check my room. He didn't.

I stayed behind the sofa for what seemed like an hour, but was in fact only about ten minutes. When it seemed safe to move, I walked quietly across to the cupboard and felt for the keys and papers I'd seen when the light was on. I picked them up and moved over to the window, and looked at them in the moonlight.

I was surprised to find that there were two sets of keys. One of them was my car keys, and the other looked like the house keys. I was even more surprised to find both of our passports were there, too. I put everything into my pocket. Now for Sandra, I thought.

Out in the hall I stood in the darkness, listening. I could hear nothing from upstairs. I started to move up the stairs as slowly as possible. I waited after each movement. My heart was beating loudly. Finally, I reached the top of the stairs and moved gently along to Sandra's room. I turned the key in the lock as slowly as I could, pushed the door open, moved inside and closed the door behind me. I turned the light on. Sandra sat up in bed, with her hands over her eyes.

'*Ma, che cosa* . . . ?' she said, dangerously loudly. I put my finger on my lips, and she saw it was me. I walked over to her bed and sat down beside her. We held each other for a moment.

'But how . . . ?' she started again.

'It doesn't matter now,' I whispered. 'Get dressed and put what you want into your handbag as quickly as you can. We're leaving. And don't put your shoes on.'

She did as I asked. When she was ready, I turned the light off, and we went out into the corridor. I listened for a moment. Then I locked the door and took the key out of her door and mine – anything that might buy us time later!

We moved slowly, nervously, downstairs – any noise might bring the guard or Andrea running with their guns, and our escape would be over. Once down in the kitchen we both put our shoes on and went outside. I took the house keys out of my pocket and locked the door behind me, and then I threw the keys away.

'We'll push the car down to the road,' I said to Sandra, as I opened the doors, 'so that when I start the engine it won't be so close to the house.'

Sandra agreed. We pushed the car out from between the other two cars.

'Thank goodness it's such a small car!' whispered Sandra across the roof. Gently we pushed the car out onto the road. Suddenly Sandra turned and ran back down the path and disappeared. I was alone in the dark. What was she doing? Had she decided to return to Andrea? Was she going to give me up? I was suddenly suspicious of her again. Any minute I thought a light would go on and someone would start shooting at me. I was about to get into the car when I saw Sandra coming back.

'What did you do? Where did you . . . ?' I asked.

'Quickly,' she said. 'Get into the car.'

We pushed the car a bit more and jumped in. The car hit something and my door shut very loudly. I tried to start the car. Nothing happened. It wouldn't start. We stared at each other. We were both frightened. I looked back at the house and tried to start the car again. Nothing.

A light went on and a window opened in one of the front bedrooms. A head appeared shouting something in Italian. I tried to start the car again.

'Come on!' I whispered to the car, trying a fourth time. This time it started. Just then there was a loud bang from the house and a noise at the back of the car.

'Quick!' shouted Sandra. 'They're shooting at us!'

There was another bang, and a noise on the roof of the car this time.

'Keep your head down,' I said. I kept the car headlights off until we turned the first corner. Then I put them on and drove off as fast as I could. There were more shots as we went down the road, but none of them hit the car.

Chapter 15 *South across France*

'What were you doing back there?' I shouted at Sandra. 'What were you doing? We could have been caught. They'll catch us very quickly now.' I was angry with Sandra – although, if I think about it, it was my door that shut loudly and woke them up.

In fact Sandra had saved us some time. 'I was cutting their tyres,' she said, and held up a knife.

'How did you get that?' I asked, feeling happier now.

'The guard lent it to me last night to cut up my bread and cheese,' she answered. 'I cut all four tyres on both cars, so they'll have to get them changed. I guess that gives us a couple of hours, even if they can get someone to come out and change them at this time of night.'

'You're absolutely amazing, Sandra Rovello!' I shouted.

I hadn't thought about where we should go. As we drove towards Dieppe, I asked Sandra what she thought.

'I think we still need to get back to Italy,' she said.

'OK. Italy, here we come.'

We drove south, stopping to fill up with petrol and buy something to eat and drink at the first petrol station out of the city. It was five o'clock in the morning. We were very tired but we thought we should still keep driving. Sandra slept a little and, at about one o'clock in the afternoon, we stopped again. We needed more petrol, and we needed to rest. After filling up the car with petrol and having a drink in the bar, Sandra telephoned her father to tell him what had happened. We arranged to meet at the Italian border the next day. We then moved the car over to the corner of the car park to have a rest.

'Let's rest for an hour and then we'll continue.'

I pushed the driver's seat back and was so tired I quickly fell asleep.

*　　*　　*

I awoke suddenly. Sandra was asleep beside me. I looked at my watch. 'Bloody hell!' I shouted. 'Sandra. Sandra. Wake up quickly. It's four o'clock!' She awoke with difficulty.

'What?' she said. 'What's the matter?'

'Quickly. Let's get going. It's four o'clock. We've slept too long!' I shouted.

We got ourselves ready and left at once.

'We're both exhausted after sleeping so little and having so many things to worry about,' I said to Sandra as we were driving. 'We'll be fine. I'm sure cutting their tyres bought us the sleeping time we needed. Now we can drive straight to the border.'

Chapter 16   *A motorway chase*

But we'd forgotten about the radio signal that Andrea had put on the car. We had been driving south for about twenty minutes, with the pretty line of the Mâconnais wine hills on our right side, when I saw something yellow in the distance in my mirror. As it got closer, I realised it was a yellow Fiat sports car. I had a sick feeling in my stomach.

'Sandra,' I said very quietly. 'Look behind us.'

She turned around. 'Oh no!' she said. 'But how could he have found us already?'

'Well, don't forget that his car can go about twice as fast as mine,' I answered. 'And he can also follow us with the radio signal.'

'And there's Andrea, too!' she suddenly shouted. 'Look! Behind that Belgian lorry.'

I looked in the mirror. There was the silver Mercedes just overtaking a big lorry. My heart almost stopped. What could we do now? Then I had an idea.

'Show me the map, Sandra,' I said quickly. She turned it round, and put her finger on Dijon so I could see where we were more easily.

'Right. We're not going to leave the motorway now, as planned. We're going to keep on going south on the A6 towards Lyon.'

'But why should we do that?' she asked, confused. 'Both their cars are much faster than ours.'

'That's just the point,' I explained. 'If we leave the motorway the road becomes very hilly, and this little car can't go up hills very well, so it would be very easy for them to catch us. Also, it's a much quieter road, with less police and help on it. What I'm going to do is drive as fast as I can along this flat motorway. They'll have to follow. Hopefully the police will soon notice all of these cars driving too fast. Once we see the police are following, we'll stop and you'll explain everything in your beautiful French. It's our only chance now, Sandra. Otherwise Andrea will just stop us and do what he wants.'

'But, Paul, that's very dangerous,' she said, with a worried look in her eyes.

'But it's no more dangerous than being caught by Andrea and that big guard, is it?' I asked.

'No, I suppose not,' she answered. 'But be careful, Paul.'

I kissed her cheek. Looking in the mirror I could see the guard's yellow Fiat two cars back and Andrea's Mercedes about another four cars back. I was in the middle lane, and the traffic was quite light.

'Right,' I said. 'Here we go.'

I went faster and faster. I'd never really wanted to see how fast the Metro could go – it said 180 kph on the speedometer, but I don't think I'd ever gone faster than 130 before. Soon I was driving at 170 in the fast lane of the motorway. I had my headlights on and my warning lights flashing.

'I don't think you'd better go any faster,' shouted Sandra nervously over the noise of the engine. The car obviously didn't like this very much.

'No,' I shouted back. 'This is OK. They're following.'

Both cars had moved out to follow us and were a couple of hundred metres behind, with Andrea's Mercedes just in front of the yellow Fiat now.

'And look!' shouted Sandra, excitedly pointing upwards. 'There's a police car on the bridge ahead.' I flashed my headlights several times as we came up to the bridge, hoping to get their attention.

By now Andrea was close behind me, and flashing his lights, too. When Sandra looked round, he waved his arm and pointed over to the side of the road.

'He's signalling us to move over,' she said. 'He must be mad!'

'Can you see the guard?' I asked. I could only see Andrea in my mirror.

'Yes, he's a hundred metres or so behind Andrea. And . . .' She took a deep breath. 'Paul, Paul . . . there's a police car behind, too. I can see the blue lights. Your plan's working!'

I tried to make the Metro go even faster. Ahead of me there wasn't much traffic, and any cars in front moved over into the middle lane as I flashed my lights. We were doing over 180 now. The engine was making a terrible noise and the whole car was shaking. At the next junction, Sandra saw two more police cars join in the chase.

She looked at Andrea, who was no more than twenty metres behind us, and said some terrible things about him in Italian. He signalled again. A space opened up on the inside and I changed lane without slowing my speed. Andrea followed.

Then I moved into the emergency lane, still going as

fast. The surface wasn't very good and there was a lot of tyre noise.

'Careful, Paul,' said Sandra in a loud, frightened voice, as she turned to face forward again. 'Look ahead!'

In the far distance I could see a large lorry in the emergency lane. It was getting closer very quickly.

'Oh my God!' I shouted, and started to slow down. Immediately there was a bang from behind, and my car was pushed violently. Sandra screamed and we both fell forward despite our seat-belts. Andrea had driven into the back of us when I slowed so suddenly. He had not seen what was happening ahead. I braked hard and fast, in a cloud of burning rubber and dust, but it was too late.

The Metro and I were not good enough to avoid hitting the lorry. The car turned right as it came to a stop, and the whole left-hand side of the car – Sandra's side – went hard into the back of the lorry. There was a terrible noise of metal against metal and a single long scream from Sandra. Then silence.

*   *   *

When I woke up I was lying in the back of an ambulance. I tried to sit up. I couldn't. There was a nurse there. The first thing I asked her was, 'Where's Sandra?' The serious-faced French nurse nodded her head. I fell unconscious again.

Chapter 17 *Life now*

I am sitting here now, looking out over this beautiful lake. The summer sun is going down, making long orange reflections across the water. I would like to say that, in a way, the sun went down on my life that day. There is much I could say, but I suppose I should tell you the rest of the story.

My car crashed into the back of the lorry. I had only a few small injuries, but Sandra's injuries were a bit more serious. She was in hospital for a few months and I spent most of my time by her bed.

After Andrea hit the back of my car he lost control of the Mercedes and crashed over the edge of the motorway and hit a tree. He died immediately. He was later recognised by the police as Andrea da Carta, also known as Andrew Card, and as Carter Andrews. He was known to Interpol and wanted for a number of big art robberies across Europe and America.

The guard was stopped by the French police for driving his yellow Fiat sports car too fast. They found out that he worked for Andrea, helping him to steal works of art and he was put in prison for ten years. When the house at Magreglio was searched later, a number of stolen paintings, sculptures and antique jewellery were found.

And when my car was searched carefully they found three internationally important paintings, stolen from Italy and the United States of America.

Sandra and I were allowed to go free, although the French police told me to drive more carefully in future. Later, in Italy, when all the information about Andrea and his business came out, the police agreed that Mr Rovello and his partners had been in a very difficult situation. Most of the stolen furniture and paintings were found and Mr Rovello returned to his reproduction furniture business.

As you may have guessed, Sandra and I married as soon as she was better. Unfortunately, it didn't last very long. Maybe we were just different types of people. Maybe it was the situation she and her family had got themselves into, maybe it was the terrible car accident in France . . . Whatever it was, a space grew between us after the accident that seemed to grow bigger every day.

And so a year after our marriage we agreed to spend some months living apart to see if that would help. It didn't help very much, so we decided to divorce. About a year after that Sandra married a doctor, and they moved to America.

Once again I decided to stay in Como. As with Jacky's death, I felt that I wanted to stay in Italy. Italy was one of the things that Jacky loved and I still love. Or maybe it's because Italy reminds me of Jacky that I've stayed here. So I bought this lovely old house on the edge of Lake Como. Jacky would have loved it here . . .

Now that I think of it, Jacky and I loved each other in a beautiful, innocent way . . . I still miss that love, that innocent love, even after all these years . . .

After the adventure with Sandra I continued to work for Corvo Pharmaceuticals. But soon after the divorce I started my own company. I run it from home using e-mail, the Internet, phone-calls and faxes.

These days I am mostly alone. In many ways my life has been very easy. And there has been plenty of time to think about how things work. I have thought about the relationship between humans and this earth we live on. And I have tried to understand how everything is a matter of chance . . .

A roof-tile falls.

A roof-tile stays where it is.

Cambridge English Readers

Look out for other titles in the series:

Level 4

The Amsterdam Connection
by Sue Leather
Kate Jensen travels to Amsterdam to search for the murderer of a friend. She goes to parts of the city that tourists never see, meets a man prepared to kill to hide the truth, and discovers that football can be a very dangerous game.

But Was it Murder?
by Jania Barrell
Alex Forley had everything, but now he is dead. Detective Inspector Rod Eliot wants the answers to two simple questions. Was it murder? And if so, who did it?

The Lady in White
by Colin Campbell
While John, a successful TV producer, is researching a new programme, he comes across a story about a ghostly hitch-hiker which bears similarities to events in his own life.

Nothing but the Truth
by George Kershaw
Hu is a student in Bangkok, Thailand. She has a problem with a dishonest teacher, and is unsure what to do. Eventually she realises she must tell nothing but the truth.

Level 5

Dolphin Music
by Antoinette Moses
The year is 2051. CONTROL, the government of Europe, keeps everyone happy in a virtual reality. This is a world where wonderful music made by dolphins gives everyone pleasure. When Saul Grant discovers the truth, the illusion is shattered and he sets out to free the dolphins.

All I Want
by Margaret Johnson
Alex is thirty and wants just one thing in life: her boss, Brad. But however hard she tries, things keep on going wrong for her. Then Alex discovers what it is she really wants.

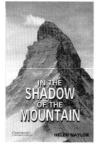

In the Shadow of the Mountain
by Helen Naylor
Clare Crowe, a journalist, travels to Switzerland to bring home the body of her grandfather, which has appeared from the bottom of a glacier 74 years after a climbing accident. Or was it an accident? Clare finds out more about her family's past than she expected and reaches decisions about her personal and professional life.

Windows of the Mind
by Frank Brennan
Each of these highly entertaining short stories centres around one of the five senses. We meet a well-known broadcaster whose blindness is her power, a war hero who hates noise and wants silence, a wine-taster who has an accident, a university lecturer who learns Tai Chi, and a magazine journalist who smells scandal and will do anything for a good story.

08710